MIDDLE-AGED WHITE GUYS

a Comedy

by Jane Martin

SAMUEL FRENCH, INC.

45 WEST 25TH STREET   NEW YORK 10010
7623 SUNSET BOULEVARD   HOLLYWOOD 90046
LONDON   *TORONTO*

IMPORTANT BILLING AND CREDIT REQUIREMENTS

All producers of MIDDLE-AGED WHITE GUYS *must* give credit to the Author of the Play in all programs distributed in connection with performances of the Play and in all instances in which the title of the Play appears for purposes of advertising, publicizing or otherwise exploiting the Play and/or a production. The name of the Author *must* also appear on a separate line, on which no other name appears, immediately following the title, and *must* appear in size of type not less than fifty percent the size of the title type.

All producers must also show the following credit in all programs or advertising distributed in connection with performances of the Play:

"World premiere at Actors Theatre of Louisville as part of the 1995 Humana Festival of New American Plays."

Actors Theatre of Louisville
The State Theatre of Kentucky
Jon Jory, Producing Director

The 19th Annual Humana Festival of New American Plays

Made possible by a generous grant from The Humana Foundation

Middle-Aged White Guys

by Jane Martin
Directed by Jon Jory

The Cast

R.V. .... Karenjune Sánchez
Roy .... John Griesemer
Clem .... Bob Burrus
Mona .... Karen Grassle
Moon .... Leo Burmester
King .... Larry Larson
Mrs. Mannering .... Anne Pitoniak

Presented by special arrangement with Alexander Speer, Trustee

Scenic Designer	Paul Owen
Costume Designer	Marcia Dixcy
Lighting Designer	Mimi Jordan Sherin
Sound Designer	Martin R. Desjardins
Properties Master	Ron Riall
Production Stage Manager	Debra Acquavella
Assistant Stage Manager	Susan M. McCarthy
Dramaturg	Michael Bigelow Dixon

Casting arranged by Laura Richin Casting with assistance from
Mark Saks Casting in Los Angeles and Jane Brody Casting in Chicago

THE CAST

ROY: *The Mayor, 48*

CLEM: *The Businessman, 47*

MOON: *The Mercenary, 46*

R.V.: *A Forerunner, 25*

MONA: *A Woman in Transition, 40*

KING: *A Messenger*

MRS. MANNERING: *Mother to the Brothers, 70*

TIME

The play is current

THE PLACE

A Dump

MIDDLE-AGED WHITE GUYS
is performed without intermission

(A small-town dump and junk yard, its mounds and valleys of debris slightly steaming in the rose of the sunset. Piles of cans, boxes, barrels, the rusted hulk of an old car, broken bedsteads, refrigerators, garbage, old signs, mounds of the unimaginable. The effect created is a dark, eccentric, contemporary hell. On top of the junked car, a young woman in a short, red dress, with a snake tattoo coiling up her left arm from wrist to shoulder, sits cross-legged. Heat lightning flashes in the distance. Far away, thunder rolls.)

R.V.: Moon? Yo, Moon, can you hear me down there? Down, down, in that river of sleep? Down with one foot in the dark continent? You remember that day, Moon? You know the one I mean. Old guy leans over, touches my tattoo, says, "Hey, Snake, we got a no-hitter goin', woman; we're workin' a virgin top of the sixth." *(Thunder)* They say there's an hour in everybody's life where all the luck you shoulda' had comes together like drops on the windshield. You ever hear that? State championship high school game, and all the luck we'd never have again just riding your arm through the late afternoon. Roy, he was four for four; Clem caught that relay bare handed for the double play. And there you were, right into the eighth, throwin' smoke and sinkers like Mr. Smooth in the bigs. And then, just then, some tanked-up dickwad on the third base side yells out, "Workin' a no-hitter, Moon!" And you froze stiff in your windup and looked over there like he woke you up from an afternoon nap, and then you shook your head and threw 14 straight, fat ones up there, and they put *five* runs on the board. I couldn't believe it, Moon. *(Thunder nearer; a dog howling)* Omens and portents. *(SHE looks at the sky)* Read 'em an' weep. *(SHE knocks on the car top)* What the hell were you doin', Moon? How come you threw it away?

(ROY MANNERING, a man in his late 40's appears over the ridge of the dump. He is dressed as Abraham Lincoln, including beard and stovepipe hat. ROY carries two six-packs of beer. He looks down and yells a name, apparently not noticing R.V.)

ROY: Clem? You here, Clem? *(To himself)* What damn color is *that* sky? *(HE takes a step forward and falls ass-over-teakettle down the dump's incline.)* Well, that's just perfect. That's just sweet as hell. Clem? *(The girl has disappeared. HE wipes at his clothes with a handkerchief.)* What is this stuff? Oh, that's perfect. *(HE pulls out a portable phone and dials.)* Mona? Mona, it's Roy. What's with the voice, Mona? You're not cryin' again, are you? Well, you better not because I'm sick of it, woman, that's why. Listen, Mona, go to the closet ... you got any mascara on your hands? Well, you wash them off, go to the closet, get my gray silk summer suit ... gray suit ... stop cryin', Mona ... run that gray suit up to the July 4th reviewing stand ... because I got nasty stuff on the Abe Lincoln suit ... Mona, I can't give the Gettysburg Address covered in dog shit. Now give that gray suit to Luellen ... my assistant Luellen ... I am not sleepin' with Luellen, Mona ... she is one year out of high school ... what the hell are you cryin' about, I put your Prozac right where you could see it. Now I need that suit, woman; you do what I tell you. *(HE cuts her off the phone.)* I can't stand that damn cryin'. *(HE dials again.)* Luellen, sweetmeat, it's Long Dong Silver. You got any word where those fireworks are? Well, those damn Chinese don't know what U.P.S. means. Well, we'll shoot what we got. Listen, I'll be there ... 40, 45 minutes, max. *(Feels beard)* Yeah, I got it on. This stick-on stuff stings like hell. Look, tell Carl keep the high school band a couple extra numbers 'cause we're missin' those Chinese fireworks. Well, you tell him to do it. I'm the damned mayor!

(Puts phone back in pocket. A man appears above. It is ROY's younger brother CLEM. HE wears overalls and a work shirt, and carries an umbrella.)

CLEM: That you, Roy?

(ROY startles.)

ROY: Damn, Clem.

CLEM: I tried not to scare you.

ROY: *(Scraping at his pants)* Look at this? What are we doin' in the dump, Clem? What the hell are we doin' here?

CLEM: We promised her, Roy. It's a sacred trust.

ROY: *(Still looking at his clothes)* A sacred trust.

CLEM: I get it. You're dressed up as a Smith Brothers cough drop.

ROY: This is Abe Lincoln, Clem.

CLEM: Oh, I see.

ROY: Seventy-five dollar rental, and I fell down the hill.

CLEM: Abe Lincoln, sure. We promised R.V. we'd come down here every 10 years.

ROY: I know that, Clem.

CLEM: Twenty years ago today. You want some Cheezits?

ROY: *(Another matter)* Clem, I got to talk to you.

CLEM: It's Mama's birthday, too.

ROY: What?

CLEM: I know, you never like to think of her dead.

ROY: Our beautiful Mama.

CLEM: 'Member how she always called you "Tiny?"

ROY: Mama's birthday! Why did she leave us, Clem?

CLEM: She died, Roy.

ROY: I know she died, goddamnit.

CLEM: Our two beautiful ladies in the heavenly choir.

ROY: I miss you, Mama!

CLEM: Mama and R.V. Makes this a sacred trust.

ROY: Alright, Clem. You hear anything from Moon?

CLEM: Can't make it. Wired R.V. a dozen white roses, just like when we did this in '84.

ROY: Well, I knew little brother wouldn't show. Where was the roses wired at?

CLEM: Liberia.

ROY: Well, brother Moon, he's seen the world. Hasn't *built* a damn thing. Hasn't *been* a damn thing. White roses every 10 years. I'm surprised he had the money.

CLEM: R.V. loved him.

ROY: She loved me.

CLEM: Well, Roy, I'd have to say ...

ROY: I don't want to hear it! Three brothers, Clem, but everybody thought he was pure gold, didn't they?

CLEM: Oh, they did.

ROY: Well, I'm the gold and you're the gold, an' he's down in Liberia washing out his clothes in a stream full of fecal matter.

CLEM: I miss old Moon. He sure does love to kill people.

ROY: He always killed things. Back in elementary, he'd kill bugs, birds, squirrels, wild dogs ... he just grew up, that's all.

Clem, I got a time problem ...

CLEM: Well, we'll do the toast.

ROY: There's somethin' else, Clem.

CLEM: What, Roy?

ROY: A real bad sign.

CLEM: Bad signs, that's right. You know that palomino horse old Gifford keeps out at four corners? Drivin' over here, seen that horse run mad, goes straight into the barbed wire, tangles himself up, goes to screamin', blood gettin' throwed up into the air, most horrible thing I ever saw, plus everybody's gettin' boils, the creek's turned red, and there's piles a dead frogs right downtown ...

ROY: *(Hands him a letter)* I'm not talkin' about that kind of sign, Clem.

CLEM: There's been three cases of rabid bats ...

ROY: Just read the letter, Clem. *(CLEM opens it)* I'm not worryin' about dead frogs or rabid bats; I'm worryin' about re-election, Clem.

CLEM: *(Referring to the letter)* So the newspaper guy knows about the chemicals?

(So what?)

ROY: What chemicals?

CLEM: *(Indicating the barrels stage right)* Well ... these ones.

ROY: They are food additives, Clem, not chemicals.

CLEM: Food additives.

ROY: I got the letter, I went over to the newspaper. Now that pissant editor has a load receipt from Long Island Petrochemical tells him how many barrels of this, how many barrels of that they sent down here.

CLEM: Food additives.

ROY: Food additives, that's right. I explained we have no barrel leakage or grounds water problem on the site. I explained the value of the contract to the city; hell, it's 37% of the municipal income, you'd think a damn moron could understand the economics, but he reads me a state statute says four of these additives - chloroethylene, hexochlorobenzine, polychlorinated biphenyls and ... somethin' else — are prohibited from interstate transport. Too much damn government, Clem, that's what it is. Now where do you think he got that load receipt?

CLEM: Well ...

ROY: You gave it to him.

CLEM: Well, he goes to our church, Roy.

ROY: You gave it to him.

CLEM: Well, he said, since it got the town so much money, just how many barrels was it? So I gave him the load receipt, and he was real impressed.

ROY: Now we got to go get it back.

CLEM: Why, Roy?

ROY: So he can't put it in the paper.

CLEM: It's just food additives, Roy.

ROY: Uh-huh, that's one thing, plus you and me set up the haulage company. You ever hear of nepotism?

CLEM: That's a positive word around here.

ROY: Never mind, Clem. Luckily you rent him the building he's in, so you got a key.

CLEM: Sure, but ...

ROY: I go get the fireworks started. I got to be there 'cause the new poll says it's a real tight race. You go pick up your key ... later on, we go on down to the newspaper, get that load receipt.

CLEM: Walk right in?

ROY: Uh-huh.

CLEM: That's not burglary?

ROY: It's fixin' the problem.

CLEM: I see.

ROY: Clem, there is America and there is not-America. America is the light. Not-America is the darkness. America isn't a place, Clem, it's an idea. Right now Clem, America isn't America, Japan is America. The problem is to get America back *in* America. Now, Clem, this is the idea that *is* America: see the problem, fix the problem, that makes a new problem, fix that problem. Whoever does that the best *is* America, and right now it's *not* America. Not-America, which right now *is* America, has two damn characteristics. Number one: fools. Fools, Clem, cannot see the problem and cannot fix the problem. These people are Democrats. Number two: idealists. These are fools who fix the wrong problem and tell the people who are fixing the right problem that they are short-sighted. For instance, Clem, let us posit this: the world's greatest bomb defuser is defusing a hydrogen bomb planted by Arabs under the Speaker's platform in the U.S. Senate. This is the only man who can defuse this bomb. He has defused bombs like this for years. Because fixing this problem is stressful, he is a chain smoker. Not-America number two, the goddamn idealists, Clem, pulls that expert defuser off the job because of the danger to the United States senators of secondary smoke, and Washington, DC blows up! We are America, Clem — you, me, we fix the problem — but the forces of darkness, the not-America number one and not-

America number two is now America, and these not-Americans are saying the *real* Americans *are* the problem, which of course *is* the problem we, as real Americans, have to fix!

CLEM: We're the real Americans, right?

ROY: That's right.

CLEM: The good ones?

ROY: That's right. *(CLEM's face crumples. HE pulls out a flask.)* Don't you dare cry, Clem. You're a big businessman.

CLEM: Then how come Evelyn left me?

ROY: Because you drank her right out of the house.

CLEM: *(Taking a hit)* I'm a bad person.

ROY: You got a haulin' business, you're into real estate. You run Gunworld, Clem, the biggest handgun retail outfit in a three-state area. You're a big success and you drive a damn Miata, how can you be a bad person?

CLEM: Evelyn still hasn't called, you know. She didn't call you, did she? How the hell am I going to raise those boys? They miss their mama. What kind of woman would run off like that and not even leave a note for those boys? How could she do that?

ROY: *(Handing him his handkerchief)* She did it because woman are a sorry damn lot, Clem. They are neurologically disadvantaged, with the objectivity of a collie dog. They hate all systems, all logic, all authority, and any damn evidence runs contrary to their damn feelings. You take out the sex drive, there isn't one man in a million would stay in a house with 'em for 48 hours. *(CLEM weeps)* Stop cryin' goddamnit.

CLEM: Jimmy Peaslee ...

ROY: What?

CLEM: His mama is the daughter of that woman used to run

the Cherokee Diner.

Roy: I got the Gettysburg Address in 20 minutes. I got some colored lawyer dead even in the polls ...

Clem: Jimmy Peaslee took a gun to school, tried to shoot his second grade teacher.

Roy: When?

Clem: Yesterday. An AK-47. He fired off a burst, but it went wild ...

Roy: Down at Lincoln Elementary?

Clem: Said his teacher was a damn lesbian.

Roy: Was she?

Clem: I think she just wore a pantsuit.

Roy: We wouldn't have this kind of problem if we had prayer in the schools, Clem. Now let's do the damn toast.

Clem: *(Heedless)* That weapon come from Gunworld. It was mine, Roy.

Roy: You sold it to the boy?

Clem: To the daddy.

Roy: So?

Clem: I feel real guilty, Roy.

(HE weeps.)

Roy: Clem, I got 1,500, maybe 2,000 people showin' up for my fireworks show, and due to the Chinese I got five, six minutes of fireworks, tops. My wife's on a cryin' jag, I got a little girl on the side is gettin' real pushy, I got to break into the newspaper, I'm runnin' against a damn minority, and my Lincoln suit is covered with dog shit. *You* don't have a problem, Clem. You sold a legal weapon to a legal daddy, and if he is so damn dumb he leaves it where Junior can get it, it sure as hell is not your fault. Democracy honors the individual, Clem, at the cost of givin' him personal responsibility, and if he can't handle the responsibility, the state ought to castrate him so he can't mess up his kid! Plus you don't even know she *wasn't* a lesbian.

CLEM: You explained that real fine, Roy.

ROY: That's right. Now I got to go to the fireworks. You meet me right after behind the Dairy Freeze. Bring the keys and a ski mask.

(HE starts out of the dump.)

CLEM: What about the sacred trust?

ROY: I don't have time for the sacred trust.

(Starts out)

CLEM: She was your wife, Roy.

ROY: That was 20 damn years ago!

CLEM: My wife left me, Roy. *(To weeping)* My Evelyn left me!

(ROY stops.)

ROY: Goddamnit Clem, you're gettin' me homicidal. *(CLEM weeps)* If I do the toast, will you stop cryin'?!

CLEM: You'll keep the sacred trust?

ROY: I will keep the goddamn, sonofabitchin' sacred trust. I'm givin' this five minutes, you understand me?

CLEM: You're a prince, Roy. You want some Cheezits?

ROY: Do it!

(HE comes back down.)

CLEM: *(Looking up)* R.V.? It's me, Clem. I'm here with Roy, in the dump. It's about 8:30. Sky's a real funny color.

ROY: You gonna do a weather report, Clem?

CLEM: Right, right.

ROY: Four minutes.

CLEM: So, R.V., it's Clem. I'm here with Roy in the dump.

ROY: You're drivin' me apeshit.

CLEM: R.V., we're here like we promised. Roy, me ... well, Moon, he's tied up with a fecal matter. Boy, I miss your shinin' face. You never loved me. Wasn't your fault. I know you loved Moon. I believe you loved Roy here ... mainly. I don't know why you killed yourself, but that was just the worst thing ever happened to me. I still wake up cryin'. You asked in that death note would we hoist a beer ever ten years on the pitcher's mound where we almost got to be state champs an' you sang the National Anthem. See, they sold the field for a dump site when they combined the high school over to Mayberry.

ROY: One minute.

CLEM: *(Quickly)* I can still hear your beautiful voice. So clear and high. Sounded like Snow White or Cinderella singin' to the mice. Boy, I miss you R.V. ... it's just a dump now, but it's a world of memories to me.

(HE weeps.)

ROY: Goddamn it, Clem. *(CLEM stops)* R.V.? You were a damn fine woman with beautiful breasts and a good sense of humor. We shouldn't have got married with you still stuck on

Moon, but that's 20-20 hindsight. You knew what a man is, but you didn't throw it in his face. You were mentally unbalanced, but you never let it show up in bed. That's a good woman in my book. *(A middle-aged woman, ROY's wife MONA, wearing only a slip, high heels and a strand of pearls around her neck, appears on the ridge behind them. SHE carries a pistol.)* You are my damn baby, R.V. honey, and any woman since you've gone is just passin' the time.

(At this moment, MONA on the ridge raises the pistol and fires down on ROY. HE and CLEM scramble.)

Roy: Hold it.
Clem: *(Simultaneously)* Don't shoot.
Mona: *(Holding ROY's gray suit on a hanger in her other hand)* You are my nightmare, Roy Mannering! *(SHE fires again)* You are a maggot b-b-born in the dung, b-burrowed down in my flesh eating me alive! I hitchhiked out here, so here's your g-g-gray suit!

(SHE flings it down into the dump.)

Roy: You hitchhiked in your underwear? *(SHE fires again)* Mona, that's enough now.
Clem: Jeeminy.
Mona: I c-curse you, Roy. I c-call demons from their d-dank c-caves and crevices the c-creatures of the night to g-give you prostate cancer and Lou G-Gehrig's disease, and make you impotent that one t-time every c-couple of months you can still get it up.

Roy: You've got to relax if you want to stop stuttering, Mona.

(SHE fires again.)

Mona: Your teenage whore assistant called me up to say you were t-taking her to the Mayor's c-c-c-c-c-conference next week. She said you b-bought her a sapphire and d-d-diamond ring. Said you were divorcing me and m-m-m-m-marrying her. She said you called me a c-c-corpse with jewelry, Roy. Well, I am. I am eaten up with l-l-loathing for m-myself, and you taught m-me that with your fiendish c-c-c-criticism and little jokes and p-patronizing ways. I looked in the mirror t-t-tonight and I saw my b-bleached b-brain an' my d-dead eyes an' I said Mona, what b-became of you? Where are you, Mona? *(The door of the junked car in the lot opens quietly, and MOON, dressed in jeans and a skull t-shirt with an army field jacket over it, boots and an old kerchief around his head, steps out. He is bearded and in every way piratical.)* I curse your sons and your sons' sons that they should be b-born without testicles, blind as newts, and they should disinter your corpse and rifle through your pockets for spare change. Now I'm going to shoot your p-puffy head off, and that will make me feel considerably better.

(SHE raises the gun again.)

Moon: *(In his left hand, he carries a stubby full automatic as if it were an extension of his arm. As she raises the gun, he speaks consolingly.)* Good evening, ma'am. *(SHE turns, pointing the gun at him)* I had a friend used to stutter until his confidence caught up with his heart.

CLEM: Moon.

MOON: How you doin'? Well ma'am, I'd have to agree with you about Roy, untutored as he is, he probably thinks you're a household appliance. He just don't know what a woman is, ma'am, and he's just unteachable as a rooster.

ROY: What the hell, Moon?

MOON: Shut up, Roy. Now ma'am, I'm a brute killer for pay, and they tell me I'm one of the dozen best shots in the world, left-handed or right. May I call you Mona? Mona, what you're holdin' there is a Rossi 518 Tiger Cat Special, accurate up to about 40 feet and, combined with your understandable emotion and inexperience you most likely won't hit me, whereas my first couple of rounds will tear off your wrist, leavin' you with one hand for the rest of your life. They tell me the pain's unendurable unless we cauterized it with fire, and by the time we got some kindlin', you'd likely bleed to death. It's strange when you can see right inside your own body like you can when an extremity's gone. We never know what we are because we're covered with skin. Once you find out, you realize we're just walkin' meat. Now I'd feel more comfortable if you'd point that thing at Roy, if you don't mind.

(SHE does)

ROY: Damn, Moon.

MOON: Well I feel a whole lot better. Much obliged. Now what can we do for you, ma'am?

MONA: K-K-K-Kill him.

ROY: Moon?

MOON: *(To ROY)* There's no punishment in death, ma'am. It's over in the blink of an eye. The thing I like least about killin' people is how easy they get off. Hell, he stole your life from you. Wouldn't you say that's the situation?

MONA: I was ... I was ... I had dreams.

MOON: Sure, I know. You got some place you could go?

MONA: Clem's wife, Evelyn, she called from Arizona.

CLEM: Arizona?

MONA: She says it's n-nice. She l-lives with the Navajos.

CLEM: My Evelyn?

MONA: She said I could c-c-come out there.

MOON: You know what you get out there, ma'am? You get yourself a shadow, so you don't get lonely.

MONA: But I don't have the money. He didn't let me work.

MOON: Well see, he is so small. He is such a small person he could only enlarge himself at your expense.

ROY: Now that's just damned well enough.

MOON: She's going to kill you, Roy, we're lookin' for alternatives.

ROY: She can't hit the side of a barn.

MOON: She isn't stuttering, Roy. Her hand's steady. You ought to hold that with two hands ma'am. Sort of like this.

(HE demonstrates. SHE changes her grip.)

ROY: Damnit!

MOON: She might get lucky, put one right up your nose.

ROY: I don't know you.

MOON: Ma'am, I believe I'm going to take up a collection, how about that? Gimme your wallets, boys. *(They don't respond.)* I said gimme your goddamn wallets! *(They throw them on the ground.)* I get real pissed off at myself, the course I've taken. I should have got into robbery, it's just so damn easy. *(Picks them up. HE looks.)* You won't mind if your pretty wife goes on a little shoppin' spree, will you, Roy? *(ROY glowers.)* So now I'm comin' up there, ma'am. Roy, throw me over your car keys, will you?

ROY: I am not givin' you my car keys.

MOON: What are you drivin' these days?

ROY: No way. No damn way.

MOON: Go ahead, ma'am, shoot him.

(SHE fires. ROY hits the ground. SHE misses.)

ROY: Goddamnit to hell. Son of a bitch.

MOON: That was about a foot left, ma'am. And if you wouldn't mind a little advice, I wouldn't go for the head, I'd go for the gut.

ROY: Alright. Alright. I'm gettin' the keys.

MOON: How are you doin', Clem?

CLEM: Well, Evelyn run off.

MOON: Sorry to hear that. You better have a drink.

CLEM: *(Pulling out the flask)* Okay, Moon.

MOON: There's a case to be made for finishin' the century blind drunk.

CLEM: Care for a dollop?

(CLEM, having taken a hit, passes the flask to MOON.)

MOON: Well, I don't mind. *(Drinks)* How about you, Mona?

MONA: *(A roar)* I hate men!

MOON: Me too, ma'am.

(Drinks)

Roy: There. *(Tosses the keys)* This is egregious damn car theft.

Moon: Tell him "shut up," ma'am.

Mona: Shut up!

Moon: Here I come now. *(Starts up toward MONA.)* Just bringin' the wallets and the car keys. Get you started, you know, before the divorce.

Mona: I was g-good at math.

Moon: Yes ma'am.

Mona: I was better than the boys.

(HE nods.)

Moon: Yes ma'am.

Mona: I could have done r-research on the universe.

Moon: Well, you're still young, ma'am.

Mona: No, I'm not. I'm dried out.

Moon: *(Puts the wallets down near her)* Well, you look a little chilly. You might like to put this around your shoulders. *(HE puts his field jacket down on the ground. HE looks off.)* Clem, are you drivin' that Mazda Miata or the Chrysler?

Clem: I'm the Mazda, Moon.

Moon: Good for you, Roy, you bought American made. Hey, Clem, would she still take 79 South and then 64 West? It's been a long time.

Clem: 64 to 44, then take Interstate 40 west all the way.

Moon: Down to Arizona?

Clem: Yes sir, headin' west.

Moon: Nice two-day drive.

MONA: I'm too old, Moon.

MOON: Ma'am, Buddha said a good fire can only be made from seasoned wood. The point isn't to end the journey, the point is to make the journey.

MONA: I made the journey with you, Roy. I thought I would rest easy and you would care for me. I knew I wasn't a beautiful, wild creature like that R.V., but I thought we could make a quiet life, Roy. That's a horse laugh. A woman's just disposable goods to you. I gave myself over an' forgot who I was, but those days are over and gone, Roy. I'm makin' my own movie now, and you're just something in the rearview mirror to me. I let your tropical fish go free in the creek; I burned your Louis L'Amour first editions, and I pushed your satellite dish off the roof. I'm an outlaw now, Roy, no one will ever treat me that way again.

MOON: Louis L'Amour would despise you, Roy. *(To ROY and CLEM)* Take off those belts! Do it!

CLEM: I don't have a belt, Moon.

MOON: Lic down on your stomachs. *(Takes off his own belt and, with ROY's, expertly belts the two brothers' hands behind them)* It took me four planes, an oxcart, and I forded a river on a man's back to get here, boys. Had to sell the gold teeth I'd been collectin' to get it done. See, I wanted to be here for R.V., do a little business, see my big brothers and take a little vacation from gettin' people down on the ground and tyin' them up with their belts. I guess it just shows, you're a prisoner of your talents. That isn't too tight, is it?

CLEM: It feels real nice, Moon.

MOON: *(Looking over HIS handiwork)* Well, okay ... *(Up to MONA)* You might want to get started, ma'am.

MONA: Are you the worst?

MOON: Beg pardon?

MONA: You have raped and pillaged and slaughtered?

MOON: More or less.

MONA: Are you the worst of men? I need a b-benchmark.

MOON: Well I don't know, ma'am. I guess I'm close enough to be competitive.

MONA: Then I'll k-keep the pistol.

MOON: Good idea. Say, you know what they do all over the world?

MONA: Who?

MOON: Those who have prevailed. Those who have brought their enemies to their knees and made them eat the dust of the road. It doesn't matter if it's Medellin or Kumasi or Kuala Lumpor, they fire their weapons in the air. They empty themselves into the universe in celebration.

(HE hands HER his automatic weapon.)

ROY: My God, are you deranged?

MOON: Go ahead, ma'am. *(MONA looks at him and then fires a long burst in the air.)* Feels good, huh?

MONA: It feels g-g-g-glorious!

(SHE hands back the automatic, keeping the pistol.)

MOON: *(SHE smiles for the first time.)* Well, you might want to get goin', ma'am. Keep your mind real empty and close to hand, that'll let it heal up. You might want to put on some clothes, but everybody's got their own way.

MONA: Good-bye, Moon.

MOON: Adios, babe.

MONA: *(SHE turns to ROY and CLEM.)* Good-bye, Clem. Good-bye, Roy. I'm sorry I was such a bad shot. I'm free now. When I'm out in Arizona, I'm going to take this money and raise b-bees. Millions of b-bees. Then with the aphrodisiac of my freedom, I will lure men to hotel rooms. I will tie them to the b-bed with silk scarves for a g-good time. Then I will place the queen b-bee on their penis and when they are completely covered with the swarm, I will leave them there to figure it out.

(SHE exits.)

MOON: Nice night, beautiful stars, minimum of snipers. That's what I call perfect conditions.

ROY: Untie me, you bastard.

MOON: How come you're dressed up like an Amish farmer, Roy?

ROY: Do you know what a divorce is goin' to cost me?

MOON: That's just overhead, Roy, it was comin' on anyway, you just have to amortize it.

CLEM: There's ants in my shirt, Moon.

MOON: I'm goin' to smoke me a Cuban cigar, Clem. They roll these babies on the inside of a beautiful woman's thigh. One of the few luxuries left.

CLEM: My wife left me too.

MOON: Everybody's wife leaves, Clem, it's a shit job.

CLEM: How am I goin' to raise my boys?

MOON: Just tell 'em to do the opposite.

CLEM: The opposite?

MOON: I wouldn't worry about it, Clem.

(MOON lights up.)

Roy: My own brother robbed me.

Moon: You can get on the phone and cancel the cards, they got all-night service.

Roy: I'm talkin' about my car! You stole my car.

Moon: A Chrysler ain't a car, Roy, it's just upholstery on wheels.

(Suddenly the dump is alive with movement. Small black shapes scurry everywhere.)

Roy: My God, what's that?

Moon: Looks like the rats are leavin' the dump, Roy.

Roy: Untie me, goddamnit.

Moon: I once saw rats eat a man alive. They ate him in circles like a corn dog.

Clem: I'm scared of rats, Moon.

Moon: *(Looks up at the stars)* You both owe me money.

(Silence falls.)

Roy: Now Moon, this isn't the time to talk about that. This is a time for three brothers, lost to each other by geography, to take hands, kneel down ...

Moon: You owe me for the fishing cabin Pop left me that you sold for me in '86.

Roy: Moon, that cabin was in bad shape.

Moon: How much did you get for it?

Roy: ... water damaged, rotted out.

Moon: How much, Roy?

Roy: Maybe $1,300, well, no, a little bit less.

Moon: You sold 1.3 acres down on the river for $1,300?

Roy: Hey little brother, this was eight years ago.

Moon: It was appraised 20 years ago at $7,500.

Roy: Are you accusing me of cheatin' my own damn family?

Moon: Yes.

Roy: There is no bond like blood, Moon, and there is nothing so despicable as to doubt it.

Clem: Mighta been $5,000, Moon.

Moon: That's good, Clem, and when you started your pawnshop I fronted you $5,000, which was ten percent of the capital.

Clem: Would you care for some Cheezits, Moon?

Moon: You sure that pawnshop didn't grow into your gun store? Because you would owe me ten cents on every dollar of profit.

Clem: No. No, the pawnshop and the gun shop, that was two completely different enterprises.

Moon: I see. You still located down on the strip across from the Pentecostal Tabernacle of Simple Faith?

Clem: Well, no, we kind of shifted over toward the water, when I changed over to family security.

Moon: Uh-huh.

Clem: Riverfront development, you know.

Moon: It wouldn't be located on 1.3 acres of riverfront property, now would it? *(Pause)* Would it, Clem?

Clem: *(Pause)* Come to think of it, Moon, Roy and me might owe you a small sum, and we'd sure like to settle up. Don't you think so, Roy?

Roy: Well, now that we think of it.

MOON: Sounds good to me, boys, because I'm thinkin' of openin' up a chain of coin laundries over in Albania.

CLEM: Albania.

MOON: Clem, those people really need their clothes done.

CLEM: Sounds like a real opportunity.

MOON: *(Rises)* Well, boys, I look forward to settlin' up.

ROY: There's nothin' that people of good will can't work out.

MOON: There better not be. *(Moves to untie them)* Say Roy, there's some barrels in the dump labeled Phinoethylbarmetholine. Don't they use that stuff in nerve gas?

ROY: *(A beat)* No, actually it's used in barbecue sauce, stuff like that.

MOON: Sure, that must be where I remembered it from.

ROY: We can work the money out, Moon.

MOON: Okay.

ROY: Well, I got a Fourth of July speech to give.

MOON: So.

ROY: I got to go *now.* Gimme your keys, Clem.

CLEM: We got to finish the sacred trust, Roy.

ROY: Goddamnit.

MOON: We got to finish the sacred trust, Roy.

ROY: You can't have your community festivities until the mayor speaks to nail down the significance. That is *democracy* which you two wouldn't know a damn thing about.

MOON: Democracy, sure. Hey, I'm out there killin' people for the free enterprise system.

ROY: You're just out there killin' people.

MOON: When you start a democracy you have to kill a few

people, if you know your history.

ROY: You don't know squat about history, Moon.

MOON: I was in Nam, man, I *am* history.

ROY: You're history alright, it was the first damn war we ever lost.

CLEM: Now hold on, Roy.

MOON: Are you mockin' my dead buddies?

CLEM: Now hold on, Moon.

ROY: I been workin' 20 years to fix what you and your buddies screwed up!

MOON: *(Starting for him)* I'm gonna rip your head off.

CLEM: *(Out of desperation)* Mama's dead.

(MOON stops in mid-charge.)

MOON: What's that?

CLEM: I didn't know if you knew Mama's dead?

MOON: When?

CLEM: July of '91. We didn't know where you were, Moon. We tried Soldier of Fortune magazine.

MOON: How'd Mama go?

CLEM: It was cancer, Moon, it wasn't too bad, she went pretty easy.

MOON: Goddamnit to hell! Was it the cigarettes?

CLEM: I don't know, Moon.

MOON: I told you to get her on to the low tar. I told you to take those Camel cigarettes away from her.

CLEM: I tried, Moon, but ...

MOON: Damn! Buried or cremated?

CLEM: Moon, I just don't think ...

MOON: Which was it?

CLEM: Creamated.

MOON: Aarrrgh! *(MOON, in a rage, slings trash across the dump.)* A man don't want his mother cremated! You understand that?

ROY: Well, she left instructions.

MOON: Instructions? Piss on the instructions! I want my Mama's grave! Where is she, goddamnit?

CLEM: Scattered.

MOON: *(Sitting down)* You made bonemeal outta my Mama.

CLEM: Well Moon, she didn't want to be a bother, see. She didn't want us worried about the upkeep. She just wanted to disperse.

MOON: You two morons went and dispersed her?

ROY: Well, we ...

MOON: Dispersed her *where,* damnit?

CLEM: Wendy's.

MOON: Wendy's Fast Food?

CLEM: Well, she stopped cookin' with everybody gone and she liked to go down to the Wendy's.

MOON: You spread our Mama out at a fast food restaurant?

ROY: In the daylily garden.

MOON: I can't kneel down at a fast food restaurant and ask my Mama what to do.

CLEM: Well you could, Moon.

MOON: Never mind!

CLEM: It's a real busy corner though.

MOON: I don't want to talk about it. *(Throws HIS head back)* R.V.!? The world's goin' to hell, R.V. Mama's dispersed. You're dead. Roy and Clem cheated on me. Communism wimped out. My trigger hand shakes. Where the hell are we? What the hell's goin' on?!!

CLEM: I'll get the beer.

MOON: *(A moment. HE calms.)* I still remember your smell, R.V., the curve of your thigh. I don't know why you killed yourself, but you're sure as hell well out of it. You could gentle me down, I remember that. We never got to say good-bye, so I'm here to do it. Hell, I'm only 20 years late, that's not too bad. You asked for it, an' I'm doin' it, but I tell you what, R.V., I'm tired of dead people. They're piled up, one on top of the other, everywhere you go on this planet. Damn, I'm tired of *that* smell. You an' me were two crazy sons-of-bitches, and that always gave me some comfort. I tell you one thing, R.V., I hope wherever you are you still got that red dress and that snake tattoo. *(R.V. appears again on the car behind them.)* Heaven for climate, hell for company. Let's chug these beers.

(They do. R.V. speaks from behind them.)

R.V.: Did you love me, Moon? *(The men turn, startled.)* Holy shit, you got old!

(CLEM slumps to the ground in a faint.)

MOON: Is that you, R.V.?

R.V.: It's me, Moon.

ROY: *(To MOON)* You see her, right?

MOON: I see her.

R.V.: I forgot you would get old.

ROY: Go on now, whatever you are. Go on, shoo! Shoo!

R.V.: Hello, Roy.

ROY: Looks just like the day she died.

MOON: What is it you want, R.V.?

R.V.: I bring the messenger to ... say, is Clem alright?

ROY: Damn, but she looks real to the touch.

R.V.: Real to the touch?

(SHE walks directly to MOON and involves HIM in a long kiss. ROY talks through it. CLEM moans.)

ROY: Shut up, Clem. Is she real, Moon? What's she feel like, Moon? I wouldn't do that, Moon. Hell, she could be a vampire.

MOON: *(SHE steps back from him. Their eyes are locked.)* Your lips are cold.

R.V.: I wrote you 1,200 letters in Nam. I got two postcards.

MOON: It was a bad time.

R.V.: How's the Buddha, Moon?

MOON: I lost track.

R.V.: Where'd you go when you left Nam?

MOON: Angola for awhile, Rhodesia, Ghana, Yemen, Burundi, Salvador, Somalia, a little while in the Seychelles, Afghanistan, Azerbaijan, shacked up for a time in Albania, 26 days in Cambodia, two years near Zagreb, and I was down around Liberia when this came up.

R.V.: You know I married Roy.

MOON: Damn R.V., what'd you do that for?

R.V.: I was having nightmares.

MOON: Were you drunk?

R.V.: Some of the time. Shoot, Moon, back then he was the next best thing.

ROY: Thanks a helluva damn lot.

R.V.: Beggin' your pardon, Roy.

CLEM: *(Reviving)* Roy! Roy!

ROY: *(Annoyed)* What is it, Clem?

CLEM: *(Not seeing R.V.)* She was *here,* Roy.

ROY: Clem, damn it ...

CLEM: No, no, I saw her. I saw R.V. So help me, no kiddin'. Wearin' the red dress just like the last night. I'm not foolin, Roy. *(ROY points. CLEM looks.)* Oh, my God, the graves are opening. It's the last judgment, Roy, it's on us. My God, humble yourself.

ROY: Will you be quiet, Clem?

CLEM: *(Drinks from HIS flask, sings)* "Swing lo', sweet char-i-ot, comin' for to carry me home ..."

MOON: Clem, knock that off!

R.V.: What's shakin', Clem?

CLEM: Oh my God, oh my God, oh my God, oh my God.

R.V.: *(R.V. touches him on the cheek. He quiets.)* I had Clem one time, too. I had Clem and Roy 'cause you never answered my letters.

MOON: Come on, R.V.!

ROY: Clem!?

CLEM: Oh my God, oh my God.

ROY: You didn't have Clem? Not while we were married, was it?

R.V.: It was just one time, Roy.

ROY: While we were married?

CLEM: It was just one time, Roy.

ROY: *(To CLEM)* You're my own damn blood and you screwed my wife?!

MOON: That's pretty low, R.V.

ROY: It wasn't in my house, was it?

Moon: You said you were waitin' for me.

Roy: You better answer me, Clem!

Clem: It was in the garden.

Roy: In the garden? It wasn't near Mama's daylillies, was it?

Clem: Heck no, Roy, it was over in the phlox. You were sleepin'; it didn't mean to happen.

Roy: I just can't believe this!

R.V.: Roy, you and I were hardly makin' love at all.

Roy: Worst case, we always did it once a week.

R.V.: Yeah, Tuesdays.

Roy: It wasn't only on Tuesdays.

Clem: We didn't do it on a Tuesday, Roy.

Roy: Shut up. Godawful, R.V., ol' Clem puffin' away in the missionary position.

R.V.: Not quite, Roy.

Roy: What do you mean, *not quite?*

Clem: Well, I'm double-jointed, Roy.

Roy: Goddamnit!

R.V.: He was the only one of you boys ever loved me. Why the hell are you gettin' riled up? I'm dead, for one thing. He'd bring me coffee, get me car parts, roll my joints, remember my damn birthday, and come down every night to hear me sing at the Holiday Inn. He loved me like a dog; why shouldn't he get laid one time?

Moon: Because it's Clem, damn it!

R.V.: Roy was passed out. I couldn't sleep. The moon was real orange over the hills, so I walked out into the garden and there was Clem sittin' on the bench.

Roy: You didn't go out there naked, did you?

R.V.: I went out there naked all the time. It was 3:00 AM,

who cared?

CLEM: I was just out walkin', Roy. I just sat down there for a minute.

ROY: You are a snake in the woodpile.

R.V.: We just sat there on the bench. He told me I looked like a statue in the moonlight. He said he come there some nights when we were asleep, he'd sit there and hope me and him were breathing in and out at the same time. We just sat there, whispering, with our shoulders touching, and after awhile we lay down in the phlox. You did real good, Clem.

CLEM: Thank you, R.V. You want some Cheezits?

R.V.: Sure.

ROY: Why the hell didn't you love me, R.V.? Goddamnit, I'm lovable. I'm a hard worker, ambitious, patriotic; I'm a damn fine provider, like to dance, I got a serious side. Why the hell didn't you love me?

R.V.: You're just too much man, Roy.

ROY: Well, I can't shrivel myself up to win a woman's love. I can't downsize what I am, R.V., I got to let it roll! It's like this country is what it's like. Those pissant third worlds can't stand the sheer magnificent expanse of us. They can't take their eyes off us, but they want to cut us down to size. It's tragic grandeur, that's what I got! Goddamnit, woman, you should have *loved* me!!

R.V.: It's not a function of the will, Roy.

(A moment)

MOON: You're sure you're dead, R.V.?

R.V.: Deader than hell.

CLEM: There was omens, Roy, the Gifford horse, the frogs,

the way the sky was. I must have seen 15 possum in a bunch headin' south on the highway, and a possum he travels alone.

R.V.: How about a beer, boys? A cold one for the road.

ROY: You want a beer?

R.V.: You get pretty dry when you're dead, Roy.

MOON: Get the lady a beer, will you?

ROY: I have got to get over to the ...

R.V.: You can't go, Roy, you've been chosen.

ROY: What do you mean chosen?

R.V.: Chosen, Roy. *(CLEM hands out the beer.)* How come you were sleeping in the dump, Moon?

MOON: I got in late last night. I can't sleep indoors, it makes me dream.

R.V.: Dream what?

MOON: Things I've dome.

ROY: What do you mean chosen?

MOON: Outdoors, I've been dreaming about you.

R.V.: I know. *(SHE pops the beer and proposes a toast.)* To the white man, God help him.

(CLEM, MOON and R.V. drink.)

ROY: What kind of toast is that?

MOON: Where are you, R.V.?

R.V.: Say what?

MOON: When you're not here?

R.V.: Heaven.

CLEM: Oh my Lord, there is life after death?

R.V.: Well, I'm drinkin' my beer, Clem.

CLEM: Moon, Roy, can you believe this. We're sittin' in the dump, and it's been revealed!

MOON: Take it easy, Clem.

CLEM: What do you do there? What's it like, R.V.?

R.V.: It's pure unadulterated longing. It's like you lost a leg but there's still feeling where the leg used to be. The feeling is for the life you didn't live, and you pass the time until you find some way to make yourself whole.

CLEM: Sure, but what's it like?

R.V.: The one you guys have is a celestial theme park with a thousand T.V. channels, continual sex and a 5,000 hole golf course.

ROY: Jee-sus!

R.V.: I go over sometime for the salad bar.

MOON: Are you kiddin', R.V.?

R.V.: Could be.

ROY: I said chosen for what, damnit?

MOON: How you like it up there?

R.V.: Too damn serene.

MOON: Yeah?

R.V.: I tried to kill myself up there, too. Hell, you know, just for variety. Hurled myself down the cloud canyons. Forget it. Once you're immortal, you're immortal.

MOON: Sounds like a tough gig.

R.V.: It's a perception thing, Moon. See, I only got the perception I took up there, and that just doesn't cut it, you know. I took the messenger gig because I figured you could help me out. I'm locked inside 25 years, Moon. I only get the heaven 25 years can understand. Hell, you must be close to 50. Tell me what you know.

MOON: Shoot low and shoot first.

R.V.: Goddamnit Moon, I'm not jokin'.

MOON: Who said I was jokin', R.V.?

R.V.: Move me on, Moon, don't leave me where I am.

MOON: Got me a limited perspective.

R.V.: You lived all those years and only got smaller?

MOON: I yam what I yam, babe.

R.V.: Well, damn! *(SHE kicks something across the dump.)* How come this dump's sittin' on the ball field?

ROY: The dump's the whole point, R.V.

R.V.: What point?

ROY: The point. Town was fallin' apart, R.V. The town, the job pool, the tax base.

CLEM: Dollar movie closed down.

ROY: I said to myself, Roy, what is this country based on? And by God it came to me, it's based on garbage. There is nobody in the world has the garbage we do! *(HE pulls stuff out of the dump.)* Blenders, TV's, Lazyboys, syringes! We did a little study showed that within one truck day of this town, two billion tons of garbage produced weekly. Bingo! You know where people want to put their garbage? Somewhere else, that's where. And there is no damn town in this country that is more somewhere else than we are. And I sold that idea, by God, and it saved the town. We got the dump here plus nine other locations. I'm not sayin' I can walk on water, but I'll tell you this here is a damn miracle.

R.V.: So the ball field's down there?

CLEM: Down there somewhere.

(Finishes the flask, throws it away.)

R.V.: How come you started throwin' those change ups, Moon?

MOON: How come you drove off the bridge?

R.V.: You ever been airborne in a Corvette Stingray on a cool night at 145 miles an hour?

MOON: No ma'am.

R.V.: Hang time, it's a real rush. Damn, I love speed. What was I supposed to do, Moon? Stick around, do hair stylin' at Babette's, work part-time at the Seashell Gift Shop, make chocolate chip cookies down at Suzi's Love Oven??! Blow that crap out your ear, man.

CLEM: You could sing, R.V.

R.V.: Good enough for the Holiday Inn Lounge, huh, Clem?

CLEM: I came every night.

R.V.: Bunch of drunks in bad ties, yellin' out "Moon River." Yeah, I could sing that good.

CLEM: You was pearls before swine.

R.V.: Thanks, baby. Ol' Jimmy Dean an' me, we weren't countin' on tomorrow, see? You think I'm gonna drag a broke life behind me down Main Street, like some old rusty tailpipe kickin' up sparks? Hell with that, man! That night I flew the Corvette, I put on my red dress an' I looked fine! I was wearin' the hell out of that thing, you dig? Figured it was time to go out large, so I just slipped my good lookin' legs into some red rhinestone heels and put the petal to the metal!

CLEM: We could see you go off the bridge from down at the Bob's Big Boy parkin' lot. Slow motion right across the moon.

R.V.: Sure, I could see you boys standin' still lookin' up. Hell, 20 years later you're still there. You look sad, Moon. Is it me or the bridge?

MOON: What bridge?

R.V.: Your bridge.

MOON: What the hell are you talking about?

R.V.: The bridge in Liberia.

(A beat)

MOON: How do you know that, R.V.?

R.V.: I keep track, Moon.

MOON: They why ask me?

R.V.: To see if you have the balls to tell me.

MOON: Just a bridge we held.

R.V.: Yeah?

MOON: Yeah.

R.V.: Just a bridge, huh?

MOON: Only way you could still get over into Sierra Leone. We didn't blow it 'cause we had to run transport through there once the town fell.

R.V.: Go on, Moon.

R.V. AND MOON: *(HE is unaware that SHE speaks with HIM.)* The bridge stretched out like an old rusty skeleton between two hills ...

R.V.: Tell it, Moon.

MOON: Those people ...

R.V.: Those people ...

MOON: Kept tryin' to come across it.

R.V.: That's right.

MOON: Everybody's snipers up in the hills ...

R.V.: *(In sync, SHE sees it too.)* Man in a big brown coat ...

MOON: Midday, somebody tried to run it.

R.V.: Uh-huh.

MOON: Looked like a man in a big coat. I was in the hills ..

R.V.: Uh-huh.

Moon: I fired a rifle grenade into the coat ...

R.V.: It didn't explode ...

Moon: Didn't explode, but the coat opened up and it was a woman ...

R.V. AND Moon: ... carrying a young child.

Moon: *(Hypnotized now by memory's image)* That rifle grenade nailed the child to the mother's chest ...

R.V.: Down there on the bridge ...

Moon AND R.V.: ... and they lay, mother and child, nailed together on the bridge for two days ...

Moon: See, nobody dared try to go out there and get 'em.

Moon AND R.V.: Lay there screaming ...

R.V.: On the bridge ...

Moon AND R.V.: Screaming.

Moon: Finally I took a rifle, blew up that grenade on the second shot.

R.V.: Then what, Moon?

Moon: I stayed there another day. Then I walked out, following the river. Took me three weeks.

R.V.: How come?

Moon: I figured I'd try something else.

R.V.: Like my bridge?

Moon: Your bridge?

R.V.: Right across the sky.

Moon: No thanks, R.V.

R.V.: What is it you know, Moon?

Moon: A piece of shit doesn't throw a perfect game.

Roy: You threw the damn game on purpose?

Moon: Shut up, Roy.

R.V.: It's getting late, Moon.

Moon: Could be.

R.V.: You don't have somethin' for me?

Moon: Not a damn thing.

R.V.: Well, it's time to get started, boys. *(SHE raises her arm, one finger pointing up, and there is a shattering crash of thunder. SHE raises her other arm.)* Spirits of wind, water, earth and fire, enwrap me here! *(Thunder, lightning)* I am appeared before you, sent by the lord of hosts. She who is both the tumult and the eye of the hurricane. She who throweth up continents and maketh men from the fish of the sea. Hear me. Hear me! *(The rain pours down on everyone except R.V. CLEM raises his small umbrella. ROY and MOON are drenched.)* I come at her behest to be the harbinger of her great messenger. Through him will the blind see, the broken mend and the heart be made whole. *(A powerful beam of light pours down on her.)* Great spirit, King, right hand of the all-powerful, we welcome thee! Hold onto your seats, boys, he is upon us now!

(A tremendous explosion, as if the stage had been struck in two by a lightning bolt. The rain stops. Smoke, debris and then sudden silence. ELVIS appears. He is dressed in his "suit of lights," the famous white sequined performance suit. A driving guitar riff and final chord surrounds his entrance. He is the same age as at his death.)

CLEM: My God, who are you?

ELVIS: I'm the King of the White Man, asshole, who are you?

CLEM: Elvis?

ELVIS: The Velvet Rocker, buddy, the Hillbilly Cat, the King of Western Bop.

CLEM: You thinned down, King.

ELVIS: I been dinin' on cumulus Nimbus.

ROY: Kinda lost your magnitude.

ELVIS: Well, I'm not dressed up as a Smith Brothers coughdrop. I'll tell y'all one thing, boys, there wasn't nobody, nowhere, no time, no way, ever seen a white boy move like me. They couldn't shake it where I shook it or take it where I took it. I was born with a guitar in one hand and the ruination of western civilization in the other. Y'all look a little tight there, boys, so the King's gotta get you ready to party! Heck, have some Dexedrine ... *(HE scatters hundreds of pills in a multi-colored spray from his pockets as if they were coins for the multitudes.)* Have some Tuinal, Dilaudid, Quaaludes and Demerol! Get up, or get down, get wherever you need to be to hear the *word!*

(Lightning crackles, framing HIS figure in its flash.)

CLEM: *(Picking some up)* Thanks, King.

ELVIS: Uh-huh! Hit it! *(Another crash and sizzle of lightning)* The Lord, she stood on the rim of the universe, and she did regard the earth, baby. And wherever her gaze did fall there was real bad doody goin' down. There was a sickly caste, a dread pigmentless, soulless, milky pale fungi suckin' the sustenance right out of the world, man, leavin' things undone, done badly, overlooked, overgrazed, snafued and skimmin' the cream right off the top. And who the hell was in the driver's seat takin' care of business? Buddy, it was a bunch of fat old white men, that's who it was! Greedy ol' farts livin' off the fat of the land while the land fell apart in their hands. They weren't gettin' it there, dudes! You can't rhumba in a sports car, baby. You can't do no Australian crawl in a shot glass. We had it, man, and we pissed it away! Regard me, brethren. I was the most beautiful cat ever rolled into Memphis in a '39 Plymouth. I could sing Black boogie and the Mississippi Delta blues. I could shuck and jive like a funky angel. I was the white man triumphant, baby. If I wanted it *now,* I got it *now.* I was the boss, the king, El Presidente Grande, and I ended up fat as a grain-fed hog, down on my knees on the bathroom floor with my head floatin' in a toilet bowl. Hell, you're down in the bowl with me, boys. Y'all had played errorless, no-hit ball goin' into the eighth inning, and you took it from there to the dung heap, poisoned in spirit and your women flee you into the night with whatever they can carry.

CLEM: *(Delighted)* He's talkin' about us, boys!

ELVIS: She-it, compadres! The last time the Lord saw somethin' like this, she had the game rained out, man, but the Lord wouldn't even trust you cats to build an ark! Huh-uh! She was set to hurl the white man into the eternal dark and see what somebody else could do with it. My people were goin' down, baby, the bell was tollin' the midnight hour, cats, so I had the cherubim and seraphim deliver me to the Lord's right hand an' I whipped out my guitar and shucked out a tune, boys.

CLEM: We love you, Elvis!

ELVIS: *(HE throws out his hand and an unseen band crashes into a Rock and Roll riff. ELVIS' voice is now amplified.)* I rocked it, baby, laid down a hot lick, turned it every way but loose, like you know I can, and there amongst the beatific host, the Lord, she got down, she got tight, she got right with my music, and she boogied through the day, and a night, and a day and when I sent that last reverb down through the chambers of her immortal heart, she said, "Elvis, I thought I'd seen it all when I saw Lucifer, but the way you're rockin' tonight, I'm gonna give the white man one *(echoed)* more *(echoed)* chance *(echoed)*." *(The music ends.)* And I said, "Lord, I'm hip and I'm on it, what's the deal?" And she laid her cool hand on my cheek and asked did I remember what my precious mama said to me when I done wrong and lied about it. And I said, "Yes Lord, I do." She said, "Sonny boy, there ain't nothin' done in this old world so debauched and brought low that you can't get right with your God and your mama with just two little words ... *(The big finish)* and listen here now, those two words, those two paradisiacal confections, sweet as plums or summer cherries, those two words are ... I'm sorry!"

(A pause. Distant thunder rolls. The words "I'm Sorry" echoe through the heavens.)

MOON: Hey Elvis?
ELVIS: Yeah?
MOON: The Lord God wants us to say we're sorry?
ELVIS: Uh-huh.
MOON: Just "I'm sorry?"
Elvis: Well, it's kind of a cosmic thing, man. But you got it, yeah. Otherwise she's gonna send down the white flu, let it blanket the earth, uh-huh, all you white guys sneeze yourself right into eternity inside of two weeks.
CLEM: The white flu!?
ROY: What the hell are we s'posed to have done?
ELVIS: *(HIS arms wide)* This.

Roy: Hey, everybody throws things away, okay?

Elvis: But who was runnin' the store, buddy?

Roy: Well, it wasn't me, big guy.

Elvis: Well, who the hell was it?

Roy: Hell, you got your media, your cartels, your multi-nationals, your big government.

Elvis: And who was runnin' them?

Roy: How the hell am I supposed to know?

Elvis: Well, let's just say they weren't purple, how about that?

Roy: I'm damn tired of everybody talkin' trash on the white man. Hell, we thought up about 90% of civilization. It was 12 of our own kind sat with Christ at his table. If these goddamn minorities shoulda led us somewhere, why didn't they step up to the plate!

(HE sneezes explosively.)

Elvis: Sounds like you're comin' down with somethin'. Say, R.V., how about some seraphim send us down a milkshake, maybe put an egg in it?

(R.V. snaps her fingers.)

Clem: Say, King ...

Elvis: Uh-huh?

Clem: You kinda lost me on the curve, King.

(The milkshake descends from the flies.)

Elvis: Hell, y'all explain it, R.V., I'm gonna take a load off.

(Takes the milkshake and makes himself comfortable.)

R.V.: Hear me, fisherman. *(Lightning)* You, before me, of all those assembled, are the chosen. The bellwethers, the forerunners, you hold redemption in the palm of your hand!

ELVIS: She ain't kiddin'.

R.V.: See Clem, the Lord, she asked me did I know any white guys, and I said sure.

CLEM: How come she asked you, R.V.?

R.V.: I was just standin' there. She touched my snake tattoo, filling me with light, saying I should pave the way and we should proclaim the news.

ELVIS: *(Drinking his milkshake)* Do it, iridescent one.

R.V.: Attend me, white ones! *(Sizzling lightning crash)* The Lord God, the First Cause, the Celestial She, the Big Femina, instructs you here to prepare your hearts and set out on foot from this place to great Washington Monument in the city yclept "D.C." and to carry on that journey of the spirit a sign of apology.

CLEM: Gollee Roy, we could do that!

R.V.: Your garments shall you here divest, and your journey shall be unclothed.

(A pause)

MOON: Say what?

ELVIS: You got to do it butt-naked, buddy.

ROY: Now just hold on here.

ELVIS: *(Holding out the milkshake)* You ever try one with an egg in it?

ROY: You want us to strip down and walk 600 miles from

here to D.C. with a sign says "I'm sorry?"

ELVIS: Gonna get a hella of a suntan.

ROY: When hell freezes over, boy! I'm the best damn thing genetics ever come up with, an' that's the American white man, runnin' the most powerful damn nation this world's ever seen, an' we don't strip down for some damn hallucination!

(HE sneezes.)

ELVIS: Have a Kleenex, Roy.

R.V.: Oh man, repent all and regard thee here thy immortal soul.

ROY: Damnit, Moon, listen to this.

MOON: I'm listenin'.

ROY: Clem?

CLEM: Well ...

ROY: Stand up for your own blood, goddamnit!

CLEM: I guess God's my own blood, Roy.

R.V.: Lo, the plague will descend, your bodies be consumed and your heart sundered.

MOON: I don't have a heart, R.V.

R.V.: You just never turned it on, Moon.

ROY: R.V.?

R.V.: Sinner, save your kind and rejoice, lest you and all your tribe shall perish from the earth.

MOON: You comin', Elvis?

ELVIS: I'll be just above your head, man.

MOON: You sorry?

ELVIS: I failed my precious mama. I can't sleep the eternal sleep when I done like that.

ROY: The white man shouldn't have to take the rap for this!

ELVIS: Tough nuggies, Roy.

ROY: Who the hell has the moral authority to stand here in this dump and tell me I got to take off my underpants?!

ELVIS: I was you, I'd ask your precious mama.

ROY: How the hell am I gonna ask my Mama?

MOON: You can't ask her, you damn moron, you dispersed her!

(A heavenly chord; a puff of smoke. Their mother appears on the ridge. SHE is in her early 70's, wearing a housedress. SHE has a halo.)

CLEM: Holy smoke!

MRS. MANNERING: Hello, son.

ROY AND MOON: Mama!

MRS. MANNERING: Now you do what Elvis says, Roy. I only hope to goodness you took a shower.

CLEM: It's you, Mama.

MRS. MANNERING: Hello Bootsie. I just cannot believe you let a eight-year-old child get hold of an AK-47.

CLEM: I know, Mama.

MRS. MANNERING: I believe you've been imbibing hard liquor.

CLEM: It's only 80 proof, Mama.

MRS. MANNERING: Well, you had better pull up your boot straps. Moon Mannering, what is that on your face?

MOON: Facial hair, Mama.

MRS. MANNERING: You got something to be ashamed of hid behind that mess?

MOON: Well, Mama ...

MRS. MANNERING: You better not let your father catch you like that. Do you have blood on your hands, son?

MOON: I do, Mama.

MRS. MANNERING: I ought to whip your butt off. Thou shalt not kill, do you hear me? Tiny, what in heaven's name are you got up as?

ROY: Abraham Lincoln, Mama.

MRS. MANNERING: Remember the sin of pride, Tiny. Pride goeth before a fall. Look up sinner.

(ROY does.)

CLEM: Gollee Moses.

ROY: Oh, my God, Mama. *(CLEM lets out a long whistle.)* It's the load receipt printed in fire on the sky.

CLEM: Those letters must be a mile high.

ROY: See what you did, Clem?

CLEM: It's real readable.

ROY: Shut up.

CLEM: *(Trying to make up)* You want some Cheezits?

ROY: *(Ripping them from his hand. Stomps them)* Arrrrrrgh!

CLEM: You broke my Cheezits. Those were all the Cheezits I had.

ROY: Shut up!

CLEM: *(Suddenly twisted with rage; the straw that broke the camel's back.)* Don't ... you ... tell me ... to ... shut up!! You have ... humiliated me ... for 40 years. *(HE reaches down and picks up an iron bar out of the dump.)* If you ever ... ever speak to me in that tone of voice ... Roy ... I will mash you like a potato, tear out your liver and heart and devour them, whole.

MRS. MANNERING: *(Clapping her hands as you do with children)* Now that is enough, now. You may not eat your brother. That is out of the question.

CLEM: *(Returning to himself)* Golly, Mama ... I didn't mean that.

MRS. MANNERING: Of course you didn't.

MOON: *(Looking at the sky)* Well, they know what you got in your dump all over North America now, Roy.

MRS. MANNERING: *(With finality)* People do not eat their own. *(SHE points up.)* Think of your mama seein' your dirty laundry bein' washed right across the night sky, Roy. You better get right with the deity. *(ROY hangs his head.)* Now have you boys been brushing your teeth?

THE BOYS: Yes Mama.

MRS. MANNERING: Then get undressed.

ROY: I don't want to, Mama.

MRS. MANNERING: It is very, very late.

ROY: I ... just can't ... Mama.

MRS. MANNERING: Why not, Roy?

ROY: I'm ashamed of the size of my sexual member.

MRS. MANNERING: God gave you that body, there is no reason to be ashamed of it. You think I haven't seen your thing before?

ROY: Yes Mama.

MRS. MANNERING: You have a responsibility to your fellow creatures, Roy Mannering, now I don't want to hear anymore about it. Your sweet Grandpa Abbey, 100 years old, your kind Uncle William always sent five dollars on your birthday, you want them to die of this flu?

THE BOYS: No Mama.

MRS. MANNERING: Well, I would think not. I carried you

inside me, boys, and you were, every one of you, breech
births. I have cradled your tiny fevered bodies in my arms and
sang to you from the opera Aida by the immortal Verdi. I
watched you grow from beautiful, tiny, tow-headed
perfections into big, splotchy, gangly things who
masturbated. I paid your car insurance long after it should
have been your responsibility. Yes, Jesus, I have suffered!
You could see me draining out into you like a bottle
emptying. There wasn't a drop, not a scintilla, left for my
thoughts or feelings or dreams. I could have been a supply-
side economist or the President of the United States. After
you were born, your father was afraid to have marital
relations with me because you boys never learned to knock. I
dreamed of Mr. Presley drenching my body with scented oils
and creamy peanut butter and taking his will with me, but
none of you would ever drive me to Memphis! I died as I had
lived, a housewife, a mother, a cleaning lady and, when that
time came, when I did die, when I was no longer your lifelong
wet nurse, you irresponsible sons-of-bitches dispersed me to
the wrong place!

ROY: Mama!

MRS. MANNERING: I said Hardee's, goddamnit, not
Wendy's! Wendy's Big Bacon Classic is pigeon piss
compared to Hardee's Friscoburger! I wanted to be at
Hardee's in amongst the begonias, across from the drive-thru!

CLEM: It wasn't Wendy's?

Mrs. Mannering: Never mind! That was then, this is now.
You can make it up to me *here, after death.* You can give me
what I never had, my dreams, my glory, my raison d'être.
You three, my spawn, have been chosen by the apogee, the
highest of the high, to save the white man! All is forgiven;

seize the day, do it for your mama!! *(They stand astounded.)*
Go on, I'm waiting. *(CLEM unbuttons his work shirt. ROY
and MOON are still. CLEM takes off the shirt.)* Don't make
me get the strap, Roy.

*(A beat, and then ROY sits and starts taking off his shoes.
MOON stands dead still, arms at his side.)*

R.V.: Did you ever love me, Moon?
MOON: I did.
R.V.: Then why the hell didn't you write?
MOON: I was ashamed.
R.V.: You damn fool, Moon. Look what became of us. *(HE
stands for another moment and then starts unbuckling his
belt.)* Cool.

(SHE takes a step back.)

MRS. MANNERING: Good night, R.V.
R.V.: Good night, Chlotilda.
MRS. MANNERING: I've still got ironing to do. Good night,
Clem.
CLEM: Good night, Mommy.
MRS. MANNERING: Good night, Tiny. *(ROY's hands move
instinctively in front of his genitals.)* Good night, Moon. *(HE
lifts a hand in farewell. SHE starts to exit.)* Everybody sleep
tight now.

*(Humming a hymn, SHE disappears. A harmonica,
somewhere in the universe, picks up the hymn. R.V. raises
one hand and speaks.)*

R.V.: And Lo, grace descended ...

ELVIS: ... and they divested themselves, and the harbinger said to them ...

R,V.: As you journey, oh chosen ones, men where they stand in the fields will lay down the tools of the harvest and join with you ...

ELVIS: Yeah, baby ...

R.V.: From far off will men hear your righteous tread and stream weeping from the corporate headquarters ...

ELVIS: From the condominiums and nouvelle restaurants ...

R.V.: From the universities and the oak-paneled boardrooms ...

ELVIS: Outta' Wall Street and the Silicone Valley.

R.V. AND ELVIS: See them, this multitude of white guys of a certain age: ...

ELVIS: CEO's, estate lawyers, congressmen ...

R.V.: Pediatric allergists, downsizers, aldermen ...

ELVIS: Gettin' on their Harleys and their Swiss Alpine snowmobiles, their longin' palpable ...

R.V.: Their eyes regretful, their hands joined.

ELVIS: They are comin', baby!

R.V.: The Catholics, the Jews, the Episcopalians ...

ELVIS: The down and dirty Baptists ...

R.V. AND ELVIS: And all the lesser faiths!

ELVIS: And Roy, my man, you're in the front, dude.

R.V.: You too, Moon ...

ELVIS: And Clem, you swingin' dick, you're drivin' the vanguard forward ...

R.V.: Until at last these pale multitudes envelope the Washington Monument, as the muscles surround the heart, and from their throats will spring one single cry ...

ELVIS: The cry of sins committed ...
R.V.: The cry of sins repented ...
ELVIS: The cry of old white guys everywhere ...
R.V. AND ELVIS: "I ... am ... sorry!"

(The word "sorry" echoes through the heavens. ROY's fireworks begin overhead. Three rockets in various colors illuminate those below.)

ROY: Luellen started the show.

(More fireworks)

R.V.: Oh, boys, you were beautiful that day; your crisp, cream, pin-striped uniforms against that emerald green infield. *(Rocket overhead. The brothers remove their last items of clothing.)* You boys, like music box figures, spinnin' and divin'. The endless arching beauty of that final mile-high pop-up. *(Another rocket)* You were gods, boys ...
ELVIS: Gods of summer.
R.V.: Think what you might have done?!

(A tattoo of explosions and bursts of color. The brothers are finally naked. They look up at the display. R.V. scribbles on the back of an old "For Rent" sign with her lipstick.)

CLEM: *(A particularly glorious rocket)* Ooooooo, look at that one!

(A golden light plays down the sequined rope by ELVIS. HE puts one foot in a loop at the bottom and takes hold of the

rope with one hand.)

ELVIS: We've got to get on board that resurrection express, boys. *(Making his exit)* Hail and farewell, buddies. Y'all bring it on home.

(HE is gone. A series of sharp explosions. R.V. moves down and hands the sign to MOON.)

R.V.: Let's go, boys. I'd go south on Rural 501 and then east down the turnpike. They'll be comin' that way. Hold it up, Moon. Hold it high, my darlin'! *(HE does. It says, "I'm sorry." In the distance the Mayberry High School band strikes up a traditional march; the fireworks redouble. It is the finale of ROY's display. The brothers stare out at us; MOON holds up the sign. R.V., in her red dress, stands on the remains of the car behind them.)* Fishers of men! The night is fallen, but the lark yet sings. Oh, you Euro-centric Anglo Saxons, *(They turn front.)* there is still one inning left to play!

(There is a final tattoo of airborne explosions and a dying scutter of fireworks. The Mayberry High School band plays bravely on. The lights fade.)

END OF PLAY

COSTUME PLOT

R.V.:

Underwear: Panties, red cotton
Principal Item: Dress, red velvet
Footwear: Shoes, red rhinestone heels
Make-up: Tattoo, snake, right arm

ROY:

Underwear: Boxer shorts, blue dot; T-shirt, white V-neck
Core Item: Shirt, white dress with separate stock collar;
        pants, black fake 1860's; vest, black fake 1860's
Principal Item: Coat, black fake frock (pocket for phone)
Headwear: Hat, black stovepipe
Footwear: Socks, black; Shoes, black tassel slip-ons
Accessories: Suspenders, black; Belt, black; Bow-tie, large
        black (attached to collar stock); Wristwatch, silver;
        Wedding band
Make-up: Fake beard, wart & boil
Preset offstage: Pink sweatpants (curtain call)

CLEM:

Underwear: Briefs, white
Core Item: Shirt, short-sleeve, striped "Polo"; Pants, grey
        poly/gabardine
Principal Item: Sportsjacket, grey poly
Headwear: Hat, red, gun-powder logo
Footwear: Socks, patterned; Shoes, brown, Sebago mocs-
        type
Accessories: Glasses, yellow shooting range; Wristwatch,
        wide brown leather; Wedding ring; Class ring
Preset offstage: Pink sweatpants (curtain call)

COSTUME PLOT (con't.)

MONA:

    Underwear: Bra, white; Panties, white; Garter belt, white

    Principal Item: Slip, white

    Footwear: Stockings, flesh; Shoes, black and white heels

    Accessories: Necklace, pearls; Rings, wedding and
        engagement; Earrings, pearl

    Costume Prop: ROY's grey summer suit on hanger

MOON:

    Underwear: None

    Core Item: Vest, wool, distressed; Pants, black judo

    Principal Item: Jacket, olive army

    Headwear: Headwrap, camouflage net

    Footwear: Socks, mismatched, grubby; Boots, black army

    Accessories: Glasses, red, wire-rimmed; Wristwatch,
        black; Necklaces (3); Earrings, 1 hoop; Bracelets
        (3); Belt, Guatemalan woven; Belt, army cartridge

    Preset offstage: Pink sweatpants (curtain call)

KING:

    Underwear: Dance belt, white

    Core Item: Jumpsuit, white with gold and rhinestone trim

    Footwear: Socks, white; Boots, 1970's ankle, white

    Accessories: Belt, broad white with gold and rhinestone
        trim and chains; Scarves (2), white silk; Necklace,
        rhinestone cross on chain; I.D. Bracelets (3); Rings
        (5), gold with stones

COSTUME PLOT (con't.)

MRS. MANNING:
　　Underwear: Bra and panties of choice
　　Core Item: Blouse, pastel floral; Slacks, peony polyester
　　Principal Item: Apron, "Cobbler" type, floral
　　Headwear: Hat, gardening, with halo lights
　　Footwear: Hose, knee-highs, Shoes, T-strap
　　Accessories: Gloves, gardening with vegetables; Glasses,
　　　　　　pink horn-rims; Earrings, pearl cluster; Cane,
　　　　　　walking

PROPS LIST

Page 7:   <u>Piles Of Garbage</u> *(onstage)*
Cans, boxes, barrels, fridges, garbage, old signs,
bedsteads, etc.
<u>2 Sittable Barrels, etc.</u> *(onstage)*
Placed in DS area; one SL (height 18"), one SR
(height 21½").
<u>Half-buried Barrel</u> *(onstage)*
Sittable, Placed DSC (height 7½", dia. 16½"), no
lip on the top edge, sturdy, sustains lots o' action.
<u>Old Car Hull In Dump</u> *(onstage)*
Part of set, Moon jumps on, R.V. stands, dances on,
right passenger door opens and actor steps out,
escape to backstage from rear of car.
<u>2 Dead Frogs</u> *(onstage)*
Fake, bean bag frogs, Clem kicks.

Page 8:   <u>Two 6-Packs of Beer & Clear Plastic Bags To Put</u>
  <u>6-Packs In</u> *(Roy)*
Cans in plastic ring holder, 4 opened onstage,
drunk from, Ginger ale, one six pack can be fake
(not drunk from).
<u>Portable Phone</u> *(Roy)*
Just receiver, fits in pocket, voice *not* heard through
phone, folding antenna preferred.

Page 9:   <u>Man's Umbrella</u> *(Clem)*
Opened, black, small, foldable with wrist strap
<u>Cheezits</u> *(Clem)*
In box, eaten; one box per show, Fat-free Cheezits,
box "stomped" on by Roy.

PROPS LIST (con't.)

Page 11: <u>Letter</u> *(Roy)*
In pocket, from newspaper guy about
chemicals in dump, no envelope, 3-fold letter.

Page 14: <u>Flask</u> *(Clem)*
Drunk from, thrown in dump, has H20 in it and
drunk.

Page 18: <u>Hand Pistol</u> *(Mona)*
Shoots "at" actors, shoots 6 times without
reloading, "Rossi 518 with integral sight rib and
ejector rod shroud".
<u>Gray Suit On Hanger</u> *(Roy's)*
Not worn, Mona throws into dump.

Page 19: <u>Mac 10 Automatic Rifle</u> *(Moon)*
Stubby, long burst fired into air.

Page 21: <u>Roy's Wallet</u> *(Roy)*
In pocket, thrown on ground, dressed with lots o'
cash & cards.
<u>Clem's Wallet</u> (Clem)
In pocket, thrown on ground, dressed with cash &
cards.

Page 22: <u>Car keys</u> *(Roy)*
In pocket, thrown on ground, for a Chrysler

Page 24: <u>Belts</u> *(Moon's and Roy's)*
Moon uses to tie up Clem's and Roy's hands.

Page 26: <u>Cuban Cigar, Lighter & Matches</u> *(Moon)*
To light cigar in pocket, smokes.

Page 27: <u>Rats</u> *(onstage)*
Small black shapes scurry around set.

PROPS LIST (con't.)

Page 29: <u>2 Containers Of Soft Trash</u> *(Moon)*
          Placed in DSC area, he throws both the trash
          containers & the containers, trash thrown at set,
          actors.

Page 39: <u>Blender, T.V., Lazyboy Chair, Syringes</u> *(Roy)*
          To pull out of dump?

Page 44: <u>Pills</u> *(King)*
          Hundreds, multi-colored (Good-n-Plenty & Red
          Hots), thrown from containers onstage at actors,
          eaten.

Page 47: <u>Toilet</u> *(King)*
          Sits on, in dump, (height 18").
          <u>Milkshake</u> *(King)*
          Flies in from heaven, drunk, only water in opaque
          container, with straw.

Page 49: <u>Kleenex</u> *(King)*
          Falls from grid.

Page 56: <u>"For Rent" Sign</u> *(R.V.)*
          From dump, R.V. writes "I'm sorry" on back with
          lipstick ea. show.
          <u>Red Lipstick Marker</u> *(R.V.)*
          To write on sign, gets from dump.
          <u>Red Fake Lipstick</u> *(R.V.)*
          "Uses", not real, same color as her lipstick for the
          show.

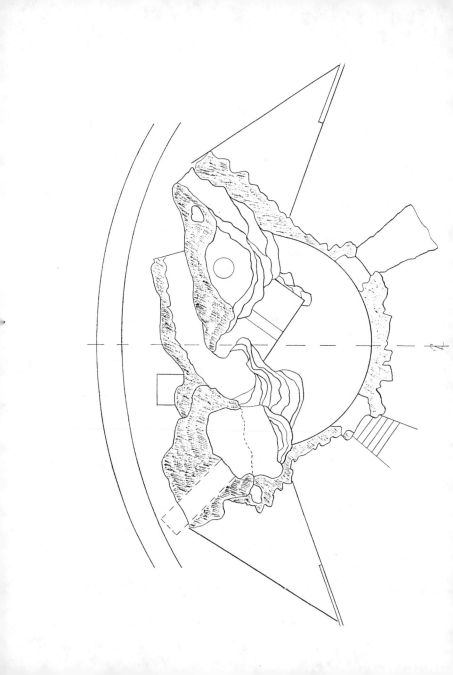